WITNESS IN STONE

ALSO BY ESTHER PHILLIPS

When Ground Doves Fly
The Stone Gatherer
Leaving Atlantis

THANKS:

I wish to thank my mother, Clarine Inniss and my siblings, Andy, Uriel, Althia, Judith, Henry, and Sherroll for their unwavering support.

My daughter, Simone and my grandchildren, Zoe, Matthew and Erin who continue to give me reason to hope and to write.

A specific appreciation to the inspiring members of Writers Ink and to all my dear friends, especially my 'sounding-boards' of long standing: Hazel Simmons-McDonald, Vivienne Roberts, Shirley Farnum, Linda M. Deane, Lauretta Hackett and Ann Hewitt.

My sincerest thanks to my publisher, Jeremy Poynting, for his faith in my work, to George Lamming for being my close friend, to Kwame Dawes who remains my very reliable critic and to Hannah Bannister for her artistic gifts.

I am grateful to Philip King for his amazing stone sculptures (at Batts Rock, St. Michael, Barbados), that appear on the cover of the book. And my gratitude to sister poet, Linda M. Deane, for the photograph.

To all the characters in the poems who helped shape my consciousness as a poet/recorder; those who are still present and those long gone, my heartfelt thanks.

ESTHER PHILLIPS

WITNESS IN STONE

PEEPAL TREE

First published in Great Britain in 2021
Reprinted in 2025
Peepal Tree Press Ltd
17 King's Avenue
Leeds LS6 1QS
UK

© Esther Phillips 2021, 2025

All rights reserved
No part of this publication may be
reproduced or transmitted in any form
without permission

ISBN: 9781845235222

EU GPSR Authorised Representative
LOGOS EUROPE,
9 rue Nicolas Poussin,
17000, LA ROCHELLE, France

10 9 8 7 6 5 4 3 2

CONTENTS

Seer	9
Drax Hall	11
Bell	13
Canvas	14
Wreaths	16
Village-Keeper	17
Rock/Stone	19
Grandmother's Crosses	21
Estate	23
Ashford Plantation	24
G, at Ninety-Two Reflects on his Mother	25
Memory	27
Black Things	29
Stairs	30
He Called for Momma	32
Stonemaster	34
Swim	36
Wing-Growing	37
Lizard	39
Erin	40
Young Rider	41
Progeny	42
Woman-Tongue Tree	43
Feathers	45
Endings	46
Rain	47
Teacher	48
Reflection at Carifesta	49
Yesterday	51
Cross-Stitching	52
Father/Self	53
Renewal	54
Lady St. Lawrence	56
Holy Thursday	58

Split	59
Director	60
Negus 2	61
Line	63
Requiem for a Lover	64
Ruminations	66
Lilies	68
Measure	69
Bless	71
Just Riffing	73
We Island People	75
Notes	78

ACKNOWLEDGEMENTS

I dedicate this collection
to our Caribbean mothers and grandmothers.

I will stand my watch
And set myself on the rampart,
And watch to see what He will say to me.
And what I will answer…

> Habakkuk 2:1
> New King James Version

The time will come
when with elation,
you will greet yourself arriving
at your own door, in your own mirror
and each will smile at the other's welcome.

> from "Love After Love", by Derek Walcott

Today I gather
these few thought stones…

These honed by the flood…
that now floors
its rankled rivers
with dry rebuttal
yet dulcet ripple tone.

> from "Some Stones May Argue Flowers", by Dana Gilkes

SEER

I'm rising, rising slowly
from age-old rock, seeing
beyond dreaming, for the first time.

How long have I slept in this cave,
its patina of centuries
dim in the drizzling light?

Where was I before my rising
upward and outward into the air
that draws me, like a remembered child,
wind sprouting wings so that I fly,
face towards the earth, trees and foliage
compliant in my soundless journeying?

Night after night I pass through ancient walls,
rooms clearer than daylight, the substance
of their absent dwellers imprinting the air.

And always this silence like an engine
that moves me – a living, knowing thing;
a chamber, invisible, all-transparent,
enfolding me.

Seeing but unseen, I linger near
but cannot hear the voices of the speakers
or their words. Only the gift of sight is mine.

> Flying near water. Fear. Panic.
> Must pull back. Change course.
> Cannot approach water.
> Turn back. I must turn back!

The silence then releases me
into the more familiar space of dream
so I come awake
and set my feet on solid ground.

Long afterwards, I learn, some spirits
crossing water never return.

DRAX HALL
for Mark McWatt

I must have learnt (aged eight
or nine) to love the dawn,
walking, skillet in hand, to fetch
the milk from Drax Hall Yard
where our grandfather kept his cows.

Chilly mornings,
hedgerows drenched in dew,
yellow creeping back
into early-late flowers,
purple peering out
from bird-vine leaves
clustered in the cut-rock
at both sides of the road;
smell of plums,
ripe guavas bursting
from the gully
filling up the air.

Once I'd passed the broken-
down mill at Waterman-Straw,
the wide sky walked with me –
pink, grey, lilac, so soft
I hardly dared to breathe
though I scarcely knew why.
But something was in that quietness,
something blackbirds and sparrows
knew, but kept their silence.
It was in the insistent song
of crickets and grasshoppers,
the whisper of khus-khus
as the wind slipped through
clouds, noiseless,

shifting shape at will –
or my creation.

This was the beginning of poetry:
this searching for the prism
hidden in the dark,
ear tuned to the pulse,
the rise and fall of the under-
growth, more telling
than the noise around us.

How could I have known my Muse
walked with me all the way
to Drax Hall Yard
on those early mornings,
when the dawn was, itself,
my first poem?

BELL

In a small country village a little girl listens
for the sound of a bicycle bell.

It's the postman arriving with his bag of letters,
and while he approaches, nothing else matters
> but the sound of that bicycle bell.

"Lord Jesus," she prays, "please let him stop here."
He's right by the neighbour. He's near… he's near,
> with the sound of his bicycle bell.

She knows that her mother is listening too,
looking for an envelope with red, white and blue
> at the sound of the bicycle bell.

But the postman hops on his bicycle once more.
No sound of his bell as he rides past their door.
> No sound of his bicycle bell.

She thinks of her father who's "over in away";
he's too far to notice, too distant to care
> for the sound of the bicycle bell.

She'll wait many evenings by the tamarind tree,
then dry all her tears so no one will see
that she's waited in vain, again and again,
> for the sound of the bicycle bell

CANVAS

We bent to enter the dark doorway.
Unlike Alice, we knew where everything was:
an old ottoman under the window,
the crooked table with an oil lamp
set to one side, the bureau leaning
in a corner bearing a few enamel plates,
cups made from empty margarine tins,
two metal spoons. We could find with
our eyes shut the one-burner Primus
stove and the smut-tot she used
when kerosene oil grew scarce.

It was none of these that kept drawing
us back. It was the piece of canvas
she'd hung to separate her living space
from where she slept in her one-room house.

When time and the damp bit chunks
out of her canvas, Miss Lewis filled
the spaces with pictures she had clipped
from magazines and old newspapers:
Greta Garbo and Marilyn Monroe capsized
us with their brilliant smiles, bright blue eyes
and shiny red lipstick. How we wanted
to be like them, blond hair and all!

John Wayne sported his cowboy hat;
Humphrey Bogart, cigar between
his teeth, starred in a film called
Casablanca – all from a place named
Hollywood, where only the beautiful
lived, and stars shone night and day.

We learnt Sir Winston, hero of World War II
lived in London, just like the Queen.
London was bombed and its bridge was broken.
We hated the horrible Hitler with his strange
moustache. He tortured Jews in something
called the concentration camps.

*

What passing stranger could have guessed
that in this tiny tumbledown dwelling,
small village children stood, not on a bare
dirt-floor, but tiptoe at the rim of the world?

WREATHS
In memory of a neighbour, Miss Lewis

She made a wreath for every dear departed
from the village: her humble offering of fern,
bachelor buttons, joseph's coat, queen-ann's
lace; red, white or yellow roses.
Small in stature, she circled the village, picking flowers
from the gardens of neighbours, their farewell gift
in memory of long friendship or shared childhood,
a young romance, some secret regret; an item
borrowed and not returned; a wrong forgiven.

She weaved with patience these unspoken mementos
into her wreaths; she who had witnessed a good many births,
watched over the goings-on in the village, intervened,
as wisdom allowed, or pressed into action by another's need.

As I return to this village, I see you after long years
making your rounds again, weaving together the seasons
of life and their passing – into another beginning.

Guardian of the Circle, *Mwenye Hekima,*
accept my gratitude in this small garland of words.

VILLAGE-KEEPER
For Miss Lewis

"Who you is? Where you come from?
Who you belong to? De Brathwaites
from Kendal? De Holligans from Wood-
land? de Batsons from Four Roads
dat move from Jordan to Cherry Grove?"

Miss Lewis claimed to be familiar
with everybody's family tree,
as if this knowledge gave the right
of passage to strangers coming through.

Not even death dodged past our village-
keeper. One particular night, from dusk
to dawn, the dogs kept howling
as if they seeing something strange.

Before daybreak, Miss Lewis knocking
at the neighbour door. "Get dat boy
to a doctor quick! I see Ma vigilant
'bout dis place las' night."
Ma dead long time!
But the mother obeyed,
and her sick child lived.

Once, Pearl Johnson, tired of her husband's
beatings, plucked up courage and laid him low
with a piece of iron. Miss Lewis seized the evidence
and kept it hidden: "Dis don't need no law
getting into it. Everyt'ing done settle."
Ol' Johnson lived but never hit his wife again.

*

Tonight I hear dogs howling constantly.
Is it you, long buried, walking through
this city? Have you come so far
to remind me who I am? Can you cover
my trespasses? Are you saying not every death
is necessary if only we would listen?

And why have the dogs gone silent now?

ROCK/STONE

Under the almond tree at the top of the road,
we ate the almonds by cracking their kernels with smooth stones.

We played Pick-ups and Jacks,
the sound of small stones scraping the steps as we picked
them up in threes and even nines and tens.

Stones served us well on our way home from school.
We threw them to lick down hog-plums at Waterman-
Straws, and tamarinds growing near the side of the road.

We shouted to the huge rock in the middle of the Quarry
as we ran by her, and she answered every
single time! They took her away to make room
for the mansions built on the ridge called "The Mount".

Just down the road in Greens where we lived
was the "Casino" or the dancing house,
the wooden building on blocks of limestone;
loudspeakers blasting "Jean and Dinah"
through the whole village on bank holidays,
women with pressed hair and bright-red lipstick
dancing with men dressed in banlon shirts
and straight-bottomed pants.

On Saturday nights there was singing
when the men in Miss Dottin's shop had up
their weekly Mount Gay rum.
With basses, descants, tenors and altos,
they turned the hymn, "Rock of Ages",
into the sweetest song I'd ever heard.

Come Good Friday, we could read our future
in the white of an egg. Our grandmother cracked

the egg, poured it into a glass and placed
it on a large flat stone in the yard.
We dreaded seeing a coffin as the egg took shape,
but a ship meant we'd travel to America or England.

At the remnants of a plantation house
at Waterman-Straws, Smitty plied his trade
in the black, stone stable as the air shimmered outside.
The only light was the white-hot fire melting the iron
he used for making horseshoes and hubs for cartwheels.
Yellow flowers from the cerasee plant climbed
a stone wall a few yards off.

We had Sunday school in the New Testament Church.
That building, too, stood on a groundsel made of limestone.
In its walls rang the praises and prayers of the old saints who,
forsaking all other ground, built their faith on the solid Rock.

Stone.
Rock.
Lasting foundations.

GRANDMOTHER'S CROSSES
In memory of my dear grandmother, Louise Hackett

My grandmother's hands were full
of crosses: her seven grandchildren,
to be exact (our mother had migrated).
Gran never flinched, just waited
for the morning cloud to break,
then she was planting eddoes,
potatoes, yams, cassava,
so seven mouths would not know hunger.

She often trekked to a nearby gully,
picking cerasee bush, bitter as gall,
to cure colds; bush-ball, vermifuge
to purge out de system; gully-root
to soothe woman-pain.

She took her produce to town
on the six o' clock bus, selling
among the sweat and market stench,
then waited in the bus-stand, basket
on head, to come home.

And I in high-school uniform, waited
(at a distance), pleats stiffened
with the starch of the cassava
she had peeled, grated, squeezed
with her own hands.
Then shame gave way to love,
and I scrambled for a seat, and yelled
for Gran to come so she could rest her weary feet.

By lamplight she talked of her young girl days:
how she'd picked pond grass for ten cents a day,
gathered dry sticks to make cooking fire,

run from the overseer who felt that his hire
included the right to "interfere" with her.

She spoke of her conversion, kneeling,
weeping in a Mission Hall,
when Jesus came and never left her heart.

In time, my grandmother shared the triumphs
of her grandchildren: one teaching,
others working in government;
studying at the university.
"Dey all do good with de help o' de Lord.
I too proud of all muh pickney!"

II

Today, I looked at the cross leading
my grandmother's casket, and thought of those
she had carried in her hands.

> Please, Granny, turn this call backwards,
> mark your turpentine cross at the door,
> turn my blue nightgown inside out,
> chant a psalm, a prayer to protect me
> from the lurking heart-man,
> from higue-ridden nights,
> the wrong turning at crossroads.

That this young man, the crucifer, now moving
down the aisle, should bear this cross with such
indifferent calm, perhaps was right.
Folding her thumb inside her palm before she died,
Gran had relinquished all.

They say I have my grandmother's hands.
I shape my crosses
               in words.

ESTATE

It's as if the limestone buildings
still standing, mostly covered by moss
and mildew, had already returned to the earth,
so deep seemed their covenant of silence.

You'd never think the noise of donkey-carts
and lorries hauling sugar-canes once filled
this yard, and the smell of syrup and molasses
sweetened the nostrils for miles around.

And you'd never know of the white man
whose skin became too white for the great house.
They built him a cottage next to the pond
where lilies stopped growing,
and only the boastful bamboos witnessed
black women brought under the threatening dark
to open their flesh to his leprous seed.

Did the wise womb refuse the damned seed,
or blood resist this dread contamination?
Or was the lazaretto, in the end, the home
for wretched souls like these?

Now, only black and white geese
float on this muddy pond
dipping, dipping for worms.

ASHFORD PLANTATION

My mother, now eighty-eight,
still talks about the sight
she witnessed as a child
while walking with her aunt
past a plantation in St. John:
small children picking pond-
grass for a living; alongside them
a woman bent double by age.

Why was this woman
still at work?
Why not at home
sitting in a rocking-chair
like her own grandmother?

This was the third gang,
too young, too weak, too old
to lead the charge in Massa's
avarice for black gold.

And so, this melding of age with innocence:
the dregs of labour exacted for a pittance.

History's wound still bleeding
to its last drop!

G, AT NINETY-TWO, REFLECTS ON HIS MOTHER

If you'd asked him about our conversation
that evening, I think he would have said:
"She listened in that still manner of hers,
when silence itself commands our fullest
attention, and like a filter, draws out
the truth as we know it,
or as we long to make it known."

He'd been reading his novel,
In the Castle of my Skin. It was the final
scenes with mother and son that had undone him;
his young indifference that so wounded him now.

"I remember she never stopped moving.
There was something anxious, even neurotic
about her… always giving some advice or warning;
speaking with one teacher after another; a great flogger,
fearful that something would go wrong with this boy,
doing all she could to set him right…
…I wish I could have my ceremony of souls."

His lips trembled with the effort to hold back his tears:

"I would tell her how sorry I am that I never understood;
that I never really thanked her for all she had done for me.
There would be all apology… all gratitude…"

He'd spoken earlier of Pa; how eager he was to present
the old man with a copy of *Castle*, to let him know
this was the book where he'd written his story.

Later, his mother said it was as if he'd handed
the old man a wreath;
as if she understood what was to come:

his final goodbye to the likes of Pa and the perils
of Creighton Village; a farewell more deep
than simple departure; the distance between
a last shared meal, and the wider world that compelled him.

This evening, he knows there is a kind of exile that is not possible.

MEMORY
for George

If sharing between two makes a memory complete,
what happens when one forgets, and every
Do you remember? is met with a blank look,
a shake of the head, *No, I don't remember...
I don't remember at all...*

Then it strikes you that you never really knew,
could not have known, the exact map of his memories;
their colours and contours, nuances; their proper indentations;
how long each stood in the queue waiting for admittance.

So, come, memories of mine, let me light candles
and burn sweet incense for you. Let me summon that day
when for the first time we sat and talked until late in the evening.
It wasn't so much what we said, but the way that trust, ever drawn
by the open heart, came in and settled itself in the room.
It was then I felt that whatever might come, I could find
such moments again, or it would be worth the seeking.

Or the way he danced with three-year old Zoë
(not knowing I observed him), but I saw how the tensions
he'd so carefully nurtured slipped for a while, his face transformed by such delight, such gentleness! I held that memory
against the harsher times when neither words nor silences
could counter disillusionment, or calm the impatience
with a world gone deaf to those ideals he'd fought for all his life.

And how his voice could turn a lecture into a symphony!
His power of intellect, the elegant phrasing rose or fell
on the under song of ocean tides, multi-tiered
resonances, the soft swell of waves, water sifting pebbles.

Where do I store a voice that caused the blood to leap inside the veins; the mind to sound out depths I'd hardly known; the ear to hear how chords, captured within a phrase, could reinterpret meaning, spark illumination.

Now I no longer ask, *Do you remember...*

BLACK THINGS

Black smoke, and the Kendal factory horn
sounding through our still-dreaming dark;
a row of distant trees, thick, silent,
not letting light through, keeping vigil
on our front house window. And of all things
our father's black Morris car he cranked
one day for the last time; it never moved again.
Only the smell of damp, vinyl, mildew,
and us children taking turns at the wheel
or gear-stick, travelling to Bridgetown
or Newcastle; anywhere or just nowhere.
And my sister weeping out some grief
we never understood.

STAIRS

There is a man who stands at the top of the stairs,
legs apart, arms folded, a stern look on his face,
none in this mansion sees him
though he's stood there many years.

A young man slumps inside his room,
his shirtfront soaked with tears.
His family mills around, helpless.
What is this gloom that nothing can erase?

They send him off to England
(the poisoned head of the stream),
so surgeons could remap his brain;
retool the limbic system — all in vain.

There is a memory that runs too deep.
It's in the wind: the whistle of the whip,
the blood-drenched earth, the gurgle
in the throat of dying men whose only

crime was in the colour of their skin;
it is the screams; the tortured innocence
of women and their helpless offspring.
Who knows why, generations later,

Fate chooses this young man to bear a guilt
he cannot name, a burden that he would not choose?
How to resolve this inner strife?
He makes his only absolution by ending his own life.

The multi-gabled roof, the casement windows
witness the bearing of his body through
the graceful arches, down the cobbled steps.
And from the stillness in the air, the trees, the earth,

arise the sighs of countless slaves
who've watched and waited through the years.

The man still stands at the top of the stairs.

HE CALLED FOR MOMMA

*In memory of George Floyd, killed in Minnesota,
USA, by a white police officer..., May, 2020*

He called for Momma, and every momma of every race:
black, white, asian, hispanic, native-american,
rose up to answer the call. But one outran them all:
she and her kind were used to running
      from the rabid slave hunter
                vicious dogs
through the underground railway
      from every street where jim crow
         deemed them nothing but worthless vagabonds.

How many nights in her head had she urged her son, "Run, run.
If they catch you they'll kill you. Take the back streets and alleys
and run, run on home."

Today she hears him calling "*Momma!*" and she's confused:
Where is his man's voice? What terror could so grip him
that he is a child again?
And she's running, running...

until she reaches the narrow but eternal bridge she cannot cross,
and there he lies, all six foot, six of him, "I... can't... breathe"

Crushed by the very thing they'd run from all their lives:

four hundred years of hate in a white man's knee on the neck
of her son —
      eight minutes
           forty-six seconds... until...
                he's... still.
She knows this kind of stillness. She's seen it many times.

*

She's holding his hand now, "Come on, son." And as they turn to go, they hear a sound as of many waters, or a mighty rushing wind: millions, millions marching around the globe. And the chant on the wind is beautiful: "*Black lives matter! What's his name? George Floyd! Justice now!*" And there's hope in their eyes as they turn to each other: One day soon, one day soon and we're done with running.

STONEMASTER

In memory of Adam Straw Waterman, an ex-slave "of pure African race"

Hewer of wood and drawer of water,
how you transformed these dire predictions!
Numbered among the dispossessed,
how could you guess the sun would never
set upon your years as "slave"?
What spirit, crossing seas and oceans,
counselled you, trained your fingers
in the alchemy that breathes in stone?
Who tuned your ear to subterranean
song only the gifted hear?

Speak, stones, bear witness!
Tell how the buffetings of wind
and hurricane could not destroy
the walls still standing here
after nearly two hundred years –
a testament to skill,
the craftsmanship
of this true son of Africa!

Say how the singing of the stones
at Mpumalanga – vibrations deep
in your ancestral memory – pulsed
through your hands that built
the St. John's Parish Church
and echoes through the walls,
blending with the organ music
Sunday after Sunday.

Playing as children in the old mill,
balancing, arms outstretched,
along a low, broken bridge;
picking up almonds under

the tree near Smitty's stone hut,
we did not know those walls, dark-
gray with age, were monuments
to hope in adversity, pride
in our ancestry, a quiet faith
that destiny will speak for those
who persevere and overcome.
Waterman-Straw — more
than a playground: the name
of a master, carving his lessons in stone.

SWIM
for three-year old Zoe

"Come, Grandma, swim!"
Not in the sea, mind you,
but on a bare, hardwood floor.
I crouch, bend over, hoping
this compromise will do.
"No, Grandma, like this!"
She's flat down on the floor,
arms and legs flailing.
I do the same, no cheating
on my little Sweetie!
For days afterwards, my hips
swing west when I intend going east.

Next time, Grandma will lie afloat
while you swim as long and as far
as you choose. Not to worry,
my arms are long enough to reach you.

One day you'll swim beyond these horizons.
In the quiet tide, lie still, like Grandma
and let the gentle waves soothe you.

But on those days when you battle
the currents that try to overwhelm you,
remember this room, how the floor,
though hard, stood firm and sure under you.
Eyes with keener vision than mine
will watch over you. And arms beyond
my reach will bear you up. Swim!

WING-GROWING

for my seven-year old grandson

Never mind, Matthew, when your sisters
put a note on their door, "No Boys Allowed."

They're growing their wings,
and need some time to figure it all out.

Last night, when you three played on the deck
at the back of the house, you were taken

by the noise of crickets and whistling frogs.
After a while your sisters grew quiet, listening,

learning the song of the moon their mothers
and grandmothers sang before them.

They knew somehow the fireflies
were not to be caught and put into a box –

not when the dancer, however stumbling her steps,
could follow the arc, the weave, the dip

and thrust of the light, could feel how life
breaks out from the womb of the night.

You won't see your sisters' wings;
a few feathers; a trail
of moon dust on the floor.

You'll sense there's something's different
in their humming, in the lighter, surer step
as they open the door.

Take this all in as best you can,
and keep it among your special memories

for when you're grown (so soon!)
and you're allowed into another room.

LIZARD

See a lizard
on the ceiling.

Approach the piano
cautiously.
Play some notes.

Watch the lizard crawl
slowly down the wall
and jump on top the piano.

You are backing off now
fingers extended
and still playing.

The lizard remains
completely still
head leaned to one side
listening.

If you hadn't run
away, scared,

you might have seen
the lizard begin
to dance.

ERIN

Your lithe limbs, green eyes
and impish grin
so easily inspire a poem!
But can any of the rules
of poetry contain you?

Take metre: already taller
than most seven-year-olds,
you beat the fastest boy
in your class in his favourite race.

As for rhythm, the day's
cycle is a bother. Your shrieks
on mornings when you won't
come down the stairs, say it all:
*Too soon. Too early. Why
does a day have to start so early?*

It's your motion that amazes!
The way you twist and stretch
past lines that limit others;
and when you turn, you blur
the senses: so quick you are, so smooth!

Sometimes wide-awake,
you're still in dreamland.
What do you see that so changes
the colour of your eyes?

Visions for which some only yearn?
What touches you and clings
so that you bring to us
a knowing beyond your years?

Erin, you are your own poem
in free verse.

YOUNG RIDER

Sunday afternoon. Across his shirt,
blazoned in blue, the words:
Ahead of the Game.
He's not among the group of boys
liming under the almond tree.
He rides alone, moves slowly
towards the intersection,
his face a calm innocence.

I fear for him:
not the threat of speeding traffic –
he seems cautious enough –
it's the warnings hidden
from his gaze;
the old signposts now broken
or discarded;
some wrong turning
he might take
in a weak and reckless moment.

How I wish him an upward journey,
and heart enough for the game ahead!

PROGENY
for Simone

You knew her in your dream;
the hand that rested firm
against your back had rubbed
your chest with Vicks
to break up fever;
brought you cooling tea
to make you sleep;
chased mosquitoes
and monsters from your bed.

Her fingerprints had patterned
your childhood world.
Now you curled into her open
palm, felt her fingers fold over you,
her hands cupping your tears.

Nestled along her lifeline,
you heard the call of ancestral blood,
and knew that countless hands had locked
themselves with hers that night.
You and the child in your womb
would be all right.
Ebe ye yie   Ebe ye yie

WOMAN-TONGUE TREE

When woman-tongue tree
dress in all-over green, she quiet,
quiet. Not a word, only bird
singing in she branches, monkey
jumping from limb to limb,
and all she doing is waving
gentle every now and then,
and that is that.

But let dry season come
when all the green drop off
and she wearing her straw-coloured
frock, then you understand
what the old folks mean
when they look you straight
in the eye and tell you,
"I old enough to say what I feel
like saying!"

Is like every wind that blow
bringing news to woman-tongue tree.
Night and day she talking: politics,
the economy, illegal drugs, gun-crime,
road accidents, technology, tourism,
terrorism, dengue fever,
chikungunya, the homeless…

Some days she get real sombre,
and talk 'bout time and patience
and cycles and seasons;
how humans got a lot to learn.

At other times is like she get a joke,
and when she start to shake wid laugh,
percussion sweet fuh days!

But then before you know it,
rainy season here again.
Woman tongue put on the same
green dress she wear last year,
and for months she get real quiet –
till time come round again
fuh talking-season.

FEATHERS

She sits in the senior citizens' home
thinking somehow of feathers: how one
should hold them lightly; how they fly –
like the four-hundred acres she once owned.

For the twenty-one-year-old bride,
life was kind, orderly as the butterfly
poised on the green grass-blade.
What warning could she read
in the sugar-cane's artful wave, or hear
in the veiled murmur of its arrows?

*They acquired our land
to build the airport; all of it!*
Then the metal-winged bird,
belly gorged with her future,
spilled its contents, indifferently,
to the far corners of the world.

How to turn it back? How to turn it all back?
How heavy her last days weigh upon her!

Pray for her a heart light
as the feathers she speaks of,
or on which she lays her head to dream.

ENDINGS

The birds' flight is laboured, so thick is the air
with the fear the living feel. As for the dead,
thousands of souls rise from their virus-ridden bodies
and hover, wingless, uncertain of their sudden journeying.
The dreaded coffin, caskets embossed with silver fittings
are precious now: they housed a final dignity, a last, loving gaze;
music and song adorned the gleaming wood.
Now, only a cold zipper runs full scale along the body-bags
heaped like dead fish, thrown into nameless graves.
Feel blessed, if in these days, you're given a jar of ashes.

RAIN
– for Linda M. Deane

Let us, in this time of drought, this Valley of Baca,
remember the season of rain, and like an anointing, let it fall
on our heads, run down our backs, soak our skin starved of feel or touch.

Let the rain on our tongues loosen syllables cracked from the dry
spit of fear, so the tongue, enlivened, may tease out dreams that cower,
uncertain of tomorrow; let us find voice to sing the world's silences.

Dig deep in the new-softened ground, find roots you have forgotten;
trace them to the tree's quiet shade. Sit there and find yourself, again.

Dig wells in the new-softened earth and learn, in the patience of darkness
and stillness, that time will come again for the drawing of water
in an abundance of sunlight.

TEACHER
for Ann Hewitt

You and D. H. Lawrence sanctioned
our romance with literature; unmasked
the tensions of love we might encounter
outside the classroom.

This morning, some fifty years since then,
I heard your meditation on the radio: Psalm 23.
Your same eye for the salient image
or metaphor, same depth, same clarity.

Only this time we're far from the coal-pits
and the industrial horrors of an England
most of us had not yet seen.
We're nearer home,

where every heart longs for green
pasture, and the greatest of minds
may yet seek the Shepherd
in the valley of the shadow of death.

Thanks, beloved teacher, for this morning's
lesson: that prayer still knits heaven and earth;
that the *Surely* of goodness and mercy
is ours if we should answer the call.

Yours still that voice that guides us now
to the greatest Teacher of all.

REFLECTION AT CARIFESTA

Thirty-odd years since last I visited
this Hilton Hotel, when, young then,
we almost turned the building right side up
with our joy, laughter, our unbound passions.

This younger crowd, emerging from the lobby,
dressed in their varied costumes, knows nothing
of those days and nights of ours, nothing at all.

I think of the tree that falls in the forest
and makes no sound because no one is there
to hear it. Is that notion all hubris on the part
of us humans, or is there an absence
so deeply felt, it's like an erasure?

Time is a slow bleed;
the bright canvas turned to dull greys;
the remnants of days that will not linger
but leap to their demise.

We look back with fading eyes
to what we'll never reconstruct —
the blocks fallen out or rearranged,
the lines stretched too thin;
where they once met at intersections,
they are crisscrossed, or broken.

And yet I like to think that from these walls,
these roots of trees, over seas and wild oceans,
above steel pan and tuk band,
that primal cry, yours and mine, still rises
high on the night wind.

For all her changing of the seasons
and her hastening of the hours,
two-handed Time will not undo her cycles
of sweet passion or of love.
Come again.

YESTERDAY

I remember yesterday...
...Anyone who had a heart...
The time is right... Turn down the lights..
...I'm forever yours...

She remembers those rent-a-tile nights,
the hardness of a body pressed to hers
when the whole world's rhythm rocked and grooved
inside one room, spread across the dance floor.

Tonight she's reaching for that feeling.
She wants it back, pure as the notes of the piano,
sharp and sure as the drumbeat she hears.

But the years have sprung undergrowth,
formed outcroppings. Her scars, healed over,
twist and bulge into once smooth pathways.

Some would say that what she's managed to pull
to herself is tattered. But now she sees otherwise:
same music, same lyrics, but a different kind of listening.
For the first time tonight she smiles, knowing.

CROSS-STITCHING
for Hazel Simmons McDonald

She sits in a corner of her wide verandah,
cross-stitching in the twilight.
She's been at it for hours, but her white
doves, lilies, the basket of fruit
on an embroidered altar cloth
must be just right. Patterns
are meant to come together.

She allows only the careful separation
of fibres, places her practised needle
into proper squares: up one, down
another in horizontal lines, starting
always at the centre, the core, the heart.

If only diligence alone could bring it all together;
stop floorboards
           from tilting,
though she knows
           they're nailed down firm;
halt the slide
           the fall out from a score just when
she thought she'd got it right.

She's off next week to the Holy Land to walk
the Via Dolorosa, hoping she'll meet *Him* there.

He'll come, the rent still in His hands and side
no stitching of hers could mend

so grace may flow to the broken wing,
the lily thirsting at its roots for water,
the answers hidden in an undue season.

FATHER / SELF

I write poems and think of my father
as he worked with wood, planing
away the excess.

He built his mahogany chairs;
I test how a word or image will bear
the weight of my meaning.

I heard him play the accordion
in his Brooklyn, New York, apartment.
Now I, too, play by ear this keyboard
that was his, using the same three chords
I'm told are building blocks in music.

I believe it is true what they say
of the threefold c(h)ord: not easily broken.

RENEWAL
for Ellice, widow of Frank Collymore

A quiet afternoon.
An elderly man and woman
in separate queues; he, bald,
wearing three-quarter sleeves,
suspenders hooked to trousers;
she, dressed in simple blouse
and skirt, grey hair in a tidy bun.
Nothing remarkable;
part of the deadening wait
for comatose bank-tellers.

She leaves her queue,
walks over, taps him softly
on the arm. He turns, *It's you!*
he exclaims, calling her by name,
after all these years!
Yes, she says, her voice a gentle quaver,
but clear, *how have you been?*

She waits, pleasantries over.

We wait as well.

I've always wanted to tell you...
she continues with a shy laugh,
I've waited all these years to tell you...

Tell him what, we wonder.

You see, Mother wouldn't let me.

The obvious? Hardly.
The meekest virgins

can get past Mother.
What, then?

That motorcycle! she says, *that fancy
red motorcycle you had back then;
you offered me a ride one day
but Mother had warned me.
You don't know how I wanted
to jump on that pillion!*

*So you wanted to?
You really wanted to!*
A grin lights his face.

Suddenly the afternoon revs up,
spreads out into green fields
and open road.
A young man rides, full-speed
leaning into the wind.

Arms clasped around his waist,
her skirt hitched up
she sits astride the pillion.
They ride eastward,
the red cycle a dervish
kicking up the dust,
tossing the years
right into the wind
like her light brown hair,
her joyous laughter!

LADY ST. LAWRENCE

Today I felt pass over me a breath of wind
from the wings of madness.
     — Charles Baudelaire

Dance is a song of the body
Either joy or pain
     — Martha Graham

Finely-drawn limbs the colour of night,
of foreday morning. Some song pours
through her, every movement a dance
only her body remembers.
Perhaps she caught some chords
deep in her belly long ago:
her first lover? Some siren spirit
from staring too long at the sea?

Some days her scarves, head-ties
are almost matching, as if her music
sleeps awhile, so that she moves,
however slowly, back to a world
where colour, shape and light
coordinate.

But then it comes; her eyes turn
inward, her body once again attentive
to a rhythm honed in unknown places.

She journeys in half-light, basket on arm,
to byways and hedges seared by drought.
There she seeks the lost, the abandoned:
fragments crusted in mud, stained
by mildew, twisted, cracked and torn.

Let her be; she gathers our discarded lives
grief-tainted, grace outworn.

Meanwhile, some song pours through her,
every movement a dance only
her body remembers.

HOLY THURSDAY
for John Robert Lee

There is a hill not far away;
close by, a village named for briars
and thorns. This Holy Thursday
he walks down the ABC Highway,
his Dolorosa.

Christ bore His cross for all to see.
But this young man, eyes mute,
seemingly senseless, bears his agony
inside an almost fleshless body,
his back still arched against the rage
of thick and twisted scars
left raw and bleeding.

The old priests placed a hand
upon the scapegoat's head
and sent it, bleating and humbled,
to the wilderness, with sin enough
to slake the thirst of vilest demons.
Could they who laid their hands upon
this man not feel the fragile skull, nor trace
a single dream still pulsing in his mind?

Beat 'e. He play 'e mad?
Beat de brute!
And so, bearing the guilt and ignorance
of the people, he walks where the road
will lead him, his gait strangely purposeful.

Who is the Stranger walking beside him?

SPLIT
for Dana Gilkes

My friend tells of the morning
she went down a short track
of her grandfather's land

picked a ripe avocado,
and on her way back
walked smack into –
                herself.

Which of the two kept on going?
Which one turned back?

I think they both re-entered
the house, only by different doors.

One peeled the fruit, sliced,
ate and licked the creamy flesh
off her fingers.

The other looked away,
grieved,
knowing
the avocado's bitter seed.

DIRECTOR

He's standing at the junction
again this morning, directing
the traffic, both arms moving
in every, and sometimes opposite
directions: left, right, up, down,
forward, backward, sideways,
crossways, in circular motion.
This man must surely be out of his mind!

Or maybe he's the trickster,
disruptor, mediator,
testing the skill, the readiness
of those arriving at an intersection;

or the philosopher
whose arms are the pages
we should look into –
lives seemingly moving forward,
but slipping backward
or simply stalled;
thoughts out of control
too far left or right;
the internal duel
that throws us
front to back of ourselves,
fearing the shadow,
not daring to trust the light.

Pause, traveller, at the crossroads
where interchange is possible:
the exchange of seeming insanity
for clearer vision, when the map
of your journey starts to unfold,
and your dead-ends
turn into thresholds.

NEGUS 2
for Kamau Brathwaite

It is
It is
how you slash and burn an entire lexicon
to rule among the harbingers of language;
how you trust yourself to the trance of words,
yet sound your oumfô for the dispossessed,
the voiceless.

It is
    evening

        now.

If only for a while,
come to this kingdom
where crows
do not fly;
the woo-dove builds
her nest in olive branches.

Here the plumed basilisk
finds no entrance,
for in these streams, forests, rivers,
webbed feet do not walk on water;
    only the wounded
        pierced by love.

Come to this Kingdom
    where dry bones sing,
    and graveyards spring
fresh flowers everywhere.

Summon Eshu, if you will,
bring Namsetoura,
black Sycorax.
Call the Orissa from the vévé;
all are welcome to this place,
for here are fountains
      and fountains of grace.

You who were born to slow the pale horses/
white deaths of our freedoms,
take your laurels now:
              leaves of the evergreen tree
              ginger lilies,
              pride of Barbados,
              bright red hibiscus

Look how fireflies glow
amidst this foliage
and how they dance
to the song on the night wind:
Kamau, Kamau,
your name will live
in the mouths of our children.

LINE

One thing they always said about him:
his work was clean. Not just the absence
of sawdust, or glue, or streaks of linseed oil
he used for polishing,

I think they meant his *line*: he could move
a point through space to where exactly
he felt it should be –

first in his head, where he practised sorting through
(to a fine art) all he considered a bother and pushed
aside whatever, whoever might clutch or cling.

He could handle the weight of mahogany.
Shape or form could not balloon or multiply
outside of his control. He'd chisel or plane
away the excess, the extraneous,
forge the kind of creation he preferred –

the upward line, the pure ideal,
the untarnished vision. Above all,

no trace or blemish of his children.
They were the warp in his precision,
the clutter,
the expendable.

REQUIEM FOR A LOVER

Other graves I have let close,
careless of the weeds un-naming them,
but yours I want to open. They say a ghost
will yield up its secrets hidden from the living.

So I lay aside your grave-clothes,
stroke my finger on your cheek,
the way I did sometimes when you were half-asleep.

Tell me, in this half-dream state,
why your heart faltered?
Was it always only like a winged bird
fluttering spaces in twilight
unsure of its homing?

I tuned my ears to songs of the wind
and learnt their cadences,
smiled when promised symphonies
were only rustlings along a drying palm leaf.

But you were the resonance of thunder.
You dared spaces to be anything but empty,
hiding with such care your sacred vows
within my hollow places, so I no longer danced
on the moon's thin edge, but was the moon herself,
a smooth unbroken surface luminous with sun and earthshine.

Tell me, why did your heart falter,
laying no claim to the shore to which it raced –
retreating, thin as gossamer on grains of sand?

If I should pitch a star to the edge of the world
I could not wake you…

so I cross your hands over your chest
and pray the folding wings
hasten the bird's flight homeward.

May the rain on this grave be gentle.

RUMINATIONS

People born in the country
are blessed;
theirs is the gift
of the beauty
of silence;
of moss-green
ponds circled
by greener shrubs
and casuarina trees;
frogs gazing
at sudden burst
of water-lillies;

the myriad shades
of green,
soft water-silk
of grass
entangling butterflies;
spiky khus-khus
guarding hedgerows,
white-seeded
candy floss waving
streaks of silver light
over miles and miles
of canefields;

of a quick glimpse
almost magical
of brilliant red berries
clustered on a vine;
the golden leaves
of coconut trees;
yellow flowers
spilling
from an old mill-top.

But most of all,
there is the soft cadence
of Nature's music,
muted, yet brilliant,
drifting into the soul;
the freeing of the senses
and knowing
that without beauty
there is no truth,
and without truth
there is no spirit;
that spirit is the spark
of life itself
reaching to all life
outside of itself;
and knowing that there's
nothing but oneness –
nothing worth
knowing
but the harmony
of all things.

LILIES

Lilies still bloom
though they weren't meant for you.
Forget the intent — where there's light
and water, any home will do.

No crystal vase suited for their display.
Breathe your apology as you cut
their elegant lengths
to fit them in a simple jar of clay.

Buds yesterday, they'll open out
tomorrow, sun or rain;
their fragrance may dispel
a distant, lingering pain.

You will remove the stem you broke
despite your special care,
then trace a petal gently
as you consider with a sigh,
whether or not they're meant for you,
all flowers die.

MEASURE

In another world we are young,
and the dark night that brought us here
has lifted. Here, there is light: the soft gold
of morning and evening mixed;
and the air, the wind, all music
we think we have not heard
before, and yet we know it.
We've heard it, half-listening,

>in the whirr of the hummingbird's wing,
>the gleeful cry of the parrot rising
>from the flower-fence tree;
>in the praise of flowers
>for the sun; roots
>for rainwater; the surge
>of tides at a full moon's call;
>the beat of a wave against rocks;
>sibilance among pebbles
>as the wave returns to the sea.

Then we remember... we remember...
we've heard this music in staccato
as the heart splintered to a dying dream.

If we could measure the dissonance
between all we had hoped for
and what we have lost
in the atonal fugue,
the contrapuntal error;
the diminuendo
to which we all must come!

But there the maestro stands;
the great conductor of all seasons

and all worlds, His baton raised,
yet strangely, still, at rest.
And in His eyes, His smile,
a perfect knowing of our every scale
and tempo; each harmony that was disrupted;
all the crescendos we have tried and failed.

And spread before Him is the perfect Score
made so by Love; by grace enhanced.

Then, *dolce, dolce,* you and I,
we dance, we dance.

BLESS

On the occasion of the unveiling of the monument erected at the Garrison Savannah in celebration of Barbados' 50th Independence anniversary, November 30, 2016

The truest pilgrimage is of the heart
that leads us home; past the metropolis,
urban landmarks, municipalities, museums –
back to this place where memory of canons,
muskets, and the tramp of marching soldiers
fades to the gentler rhythm of the Caribbean Sea.

Here the ancestors wait
for you to tell their story;
not in words, for the page may be lost,
nor in the griot's voice that may be silenced.
You must tell their history in earth, steel,
wood and stone that will endure.

Come, then, leave off antiquity – Greek, Roman,
Gothic, Renaissance – though some surrounds
you here. Lay your tools upon this altar,
this island home of coral, clay and limestone,
and may the spirits, as they gather, anoint you.

Bring your offering,
your art, your treasures of the mind
and spirit, for they will speak
a greater truth of who we are.
Bring your headlines that reveal
our triumphs and our struggles,
the ever-present war between
our greater and our lesser angels.
Capture the beauty of our sea

and sand and sky in film or song
against the tyranny of politics
or time's oblivion.
And store them, like a seed
encapsulated,
under the heart
of the Trident.

Fifty years hence,
when some who now bear witness
to this moment are one with the earth,
another generation will transplant this seed,

and as they shelter underneath the branches,
may they hear our voices rising on the wind
to greet and guide them –
we the ancestors in the making –
may the fruit of our legacy sustain them.

Bless the mind that has conceived
this monument,
and the hands that build.
Bless!

JUST RIFFING

Sometimes I get frighten'
that I losing my true rhythm,
like if I standing still
outside my heart,
hearing it beating
in iambic meter,
unrhymed trimeter.

When I feel I hearing kaiso
bursting through Miami palm trees,
steel-pan sweet like cane-juice
rippling through the evening breeze,
my heart want to leap like RPB lyrics,
flow strong and smooth as Gwyneth
Squires doing the Sailor Dance,
but I holding it back in quatrains,
end-stopped lines, half-rhymes.

Look! I come from tuk-band land,
ragga-soca land, calypso country.
I come from a place
where we measure morning
by cocks crowing in backyards,
pick up rhythms in raindrops
drumming on galvanise roof-tops,
sense the length of a line
in the sighing of casuarinas.
We learn the harmony of syllables
singing through cane fields,
hear women birthing
the spirit of blues in Mission Halls.

I come from a place
where God borrow colours

from Eden days, mix them
with crystal water nearest the throne,
then pour them 'cross the sky
over Bathsheba for sunrise.

This is a place where the foam
over reefs is white as the bones
of my ancestors;
the green of the sea is the grief
of memory, and gladness of limola
trees in brilliant sunlight.

We learn a day's diminuendo
in the flight of a firefly,
the chorus of crickets
on rainy evenings.

But for now,
I just here meterizing,
metaphorising,
just improvising –

just riffin'

WE ISLAND PEOPLE

> *...these groined caves with barnacles*
> *pitted like stone*
> *are our cathedrals*
>   — Derek Walcott

We who have few caves, hills,
mountains, in which to hide;
shut in by sea and ocean.
No piece of rock or earth
to join us to another place.
Walk far enough,
nothing but water
everywhere, everywhere.

And so we circle inward,
become our own caves;
relish the darkness,
unmask,
slough off
the outward skin;
feel the damp air cool
the burn of public gaze,
the too close scrutiny
that claims its right to know;
to gauge the best
or worst of our intentions.

We are also hills,
and even mountains.
We have crossed oceans,
known the thrust and heave
that pushed out islands,
formed this rock
that we call home.

Out of the fault
of our history,
cracks, fissures,
smouldering debris;
out of the encrustations
of ancestral memory
we build until we rise
above the surface of the earth.
We are island people.
We walk and talk the rhythms
of seas and oceans.
We flash a smile;
you see the white of reefs.
The vibrancy of bougainvillea,
brilliance of the red flamboyant
are in our laughter.

Our sighing is the wind
in casuarinas.
The salt of the sea
is in our tears.
Our weeping is the cry
of children drowned
in the Middle Passage;
a people severed
from the Motherland
with suffering as their daily bread.

We are island people.
Withhold your bounty,
we'll not die. Not now,
not now when we have learnt
to trace the drying stream
to the head of the spring,
or tap the clouds
until they pour down rain.

Not now, not when we know
that while our tongues
are quick to shape the syllables
of foreign nations,
the song of the heart
will always find its roots,
its rhythms, the syncopation
of its truest joys and sorrows
here in these caves, hills
and mountains,
these streams and rivers,
seas and oceans
running deep
inside the veins, the blood
of these our island people.

NOTES

p. 11: "Drax Hall": one of the first estates to cultivate sugar cane in Barbados in the 1650s. Built in the Jacobean style, Drax Hall plantation house is believed to be the oldest on the island. The current owner, Richard Drax, is a British MP and one of the biggest landowners in England, land bought with the profits of West Indian slavery. Sir Hillary Beckles has calculated that close to 30,000 enslaved people died on the Drax plantations over nearly 200 years.

p. 14: "Canvas": The Mighty Sparrow (Slinger Francisco) is a world-famous Trinidadian calypsonian. He was born on the island of Grenada.

p. 16: "Wreaths": *Mwenye Hekima:* Wise One

p. 18: "Village-Keeper": According to local belief, the howling of dogs at night meant that ghosts or "duppies" were around. One of the reasons for their presence was to welcome and escort their newly dead family members to the spirit realm.

p. 21: "Grandmother's Crosses": stanza 2 refers to local herbs used as medicines. Other references on p. 22 are to practices based on folklore. The word "call" in the same stanza is a play on the word "caul". Superstition had it that the caul on the face of a newborn had to be removed backwards so as to protect the child from evil spirits.

p. 23: "Estate": The Lazaretto was a medical facility set up in Black Rock, St. Michael, in the early 20th century for the purpose of housing patients suffering from Hansen's disease commonly known as leprosy.

p. 24: "Ashford Plantation": While an old age pension was instituted by the Barbados government in the 1930s, if a woman's birth was not registered, she did not qualify to receive it. These unfortunate individuals often had no choice but to work long after they were really able.

p. 29: "Black Things": Here a Morris Minor car.

p. 30: "Stairs": A famous feature of the Drax Hall great house is its staircase made of mastic wood.

p. 32: "Stonemaster": Adam Straw Waterman was a formerly enslaved man, freed before emancipation and apprenticed to a master mason. Waterman was a skilled builder. The landmark St. John's Parish Church was among the structures he assisted in building. His remains are buried in the graveyard of the St. George Parish Church, Barbados.

p. 44: "Rain": Valley of Baca, Psalm 84: 6, NKJV – a place of dryness or even of weeping.

p. 51: "Renewal": Ellice Collymore is the widow of the late Frank Collymore, esteemed editor (1945 -1975) of the iconic *Bim* literary magazine, now renamed BIM: Arts for the 21st Century.

p. 68: "Bless": This poem was commissioned by the Barbados Government to mark the fiftieth anniversary (30 November 2016) of the island's Independence. A monument was erected at the Garrison Savannah in order to commemorate the occasion. Taisha Carrington, a young female engineering student, was the winner of the design competition.

ABOUT THE AUTHOR

Esther Phillips won a James Michener fellowship to the University of Miami where she gained an MFA degree in Creative Writing, 1999. She won the Alfred Boas Poetry Prize of the Academy of American Poets for her poetry collection/thesis and went on to win the Frank Collymore Literary Endowment Award in 2001. Her publications are: Chapbook, *La Montee* (UWI, 1983); *When Ground Doves Fly* (Ian Randle Publishers, Kingston, 2003); *The Stone Gatherer* (Peepal Tree Press, 2009) and *Leaving Atlantis* (2015). Esther Phillips represented Barbados at the Poetry Parnassus Festival in London, 2012 and her poem "Word," was selected by BBC Scotland to represent her country at the 2014 Commonwealth Games. She has read her work at various literary festivals, including Calabash, in 2009 and her poems appear in several anthologies, including *Poetas de caribe anglophono* (Casa de las Americas, 2011) and *Give the Ball to the Poet* (Cambridge-Homerton, 2014)). Esther Phillips is editor of *Bim: Arts for the 21st Century* and is founder of Writers Ink Inc. as well as the Bim Literary Festival & Book Fair. In 2014, Esther Phillips' poetry was recorded for the Poetry Archive, U.K., where you can hear her reading. In 2018 she was appointed Barbados's first Poet Laureate. She lives in Barbados.

ALSO BY ESTHER PHILLIPS

The Stone Gatherer
ISBN: 9781845230852; pp. 64; pub. 2009

There is a candour to Esther Phillips's affecting collection of poems that can be quite disarming. In poems that undress the foibles of family – a father's masks and a mother's 'fortissimo' – there is tenderness and affection despite the pain. Here is a poet's voice that seeks and finds grace notes in the spaces between experience.

Hers is a poetics that locates itself in the landscape of Barbados, displaying a facility for the Barbadian dialect and the lyrical West Indian English of the major poets that have come before her. The collection's structure is a woman-centred movement of poems that begins with the complex coming-of-age journey of a child, through an adulthood of romance and crushed emotions, through the rewards and anxieties of motherhood, to the contemplative and reflective place of maturity where a woman assumes the role of elder, protector of the community, and of prophet. Phillips embraces all of these roles in her poems, allowing us to enjoy what becomes an expansive narrative through time and life's changes. She shows herself to have the wit and intelligence of an artist committed to the use of verse to test the meaning of experience. And yet in all of this, we are often most struck by Phillips's eye for detail, her sense of landscape and her willingness to locate her poems in the world that moves and breathes around her.

In *The Stone Gatherer*, one has the sense of an artist collecting stones of different shapes and dimensions, arranging them in such a way that there is space enough for them to breathe and for us to pause to think and feel.

Leaving Atlantis
ISBN: 9781845233143; pp. 64; pub. 2015

This is a suite of poems that explores the unstable territory between public and private. They are addressed to the great Barbadian novelist and thinker, George Lamming, the silent but speaking partner in a relationship of love that comes between two writers when "your flag is flying at half-mast". The suite works at multiple levels, as a record of the negotiation of feelings, permissions, exclusions and treaties between two persons who have to confront the reality of long lives that have accumulated "memories I cannot share", and not least that the poet is a woman of deep religious faith, and the man a lifelong Marxist and non-believer. What the poems also deal with in a moving but resolutely unsentimental way is the fact that the age of one of the partners makes the temporal finiteness of the relationship a matter of acute awareness. What is the poet to think when she sees the man throwing out and putting his papers in order? "Clearing out?"

The poems also meditate on the ironies of a relationship with a man who has both been public property as a writer and a leader of the struggle for Caribbean sovereignty, but also an intensely private person, habituated to a life of movement and temporariness. Quite literally, *Leaving Atlantis* references the moment when the writer is forced to leave, with a rude absence of notice, the hotel at Bathsheba on the Atlantic coast of Barbados, his refuge for many years. Is the relationship and provision of a home a "Coming Home", the arrival at a place of rest after the turbulence of a life of struggle, or does it threaten a loss of autonomy after a life of privacy and independence? What of sovereignty now when "I am your dotage, your vulnerable/ season"?

More than a portrait, fascinating and intimate as it is, of a public man; more than an exploration of the writing of the man for clues about what he might be thinking (and an acceptance of the ultimate mystery and unknowability of the intimate other), this is a suite of poems about the miracle of love, and how it may come at any time.